WHEN GOD TOLD US HIS NAME

Words by Norman C. Habel
Pictures by Jim Roberts

P A PURPLE PUZZLE TREE BOOK

COPYRIGHT © 1971
CONCORDIA PUBLISHING HOUSE
ST. LOUIS, MISSOURI
CONCORDIA PUBLISHING HOUSE LTD.,
LONDON, E. C. 1
MANUFACTURED IN THE
UNITED STATES OF AMERICA
ALL RIGHTS RESERVED
ISBN 0-570-06509-7

Concordia Publishing House

What's your name, my little friend?
David, John, or Dan?
Rachel, Jill, or Sally Jane?
Or maybe Mary Ann?

Do you know your secret name,
a secret that is true?
The meaning hidden in your name
is really part of you.

If your name is Simon, son,
it means you're like a dog,
a wild and tough and clever dog
who fears no other dog.

If your name is Fern, my girl,
you're like a plant that sings
with very dainty, pretty leaves
that look like fairies' wings.

If your name is Robyn, child,
you're like a bird so dear,
a gentle little singing bird
who tells us spring is here.

I'm sure you know the names
of many, many kids.
But do you know the names of kings
or the secret name of God?

I'm sure you must remember
how the leopard got his spots.
But do you know the story
of how God got His name?

Let me tell you all about the day
when God told us His secret name.

It all started years ago
in the far-off land of Egypt,
where all God's people lived,
far away from home.

Now it happened that there rose
a mighty king in Egypt,
who hated all God's people,
the family of Jacob,
and made them all his slaves.

He made them mix up mud with straw
to made mud bricks for him.
Day after day they stomped
in the mud,
the shlurpy mud,
the shloppy mud,
the shlurpy, shloppy, shloupy mud
that gurgles,
GLUB GLUB GLUB GLUB GLUB

Do you like to play in mud,
the way that most kids do?
Did you ever sing the puddle song?
Shall I sing it once for you?

"Muddy puddle!
Muddy puddle!
Muddy puddle ooooh!
It's fun to muddle
in the puddle
when it sticks to you!"

But the children of God in Egypt
hated all that mud,
and they didn't sing that song
quite the way we do.

"Muddy puddle!
Muddy puddle!
Muddy puddle oooooh!
We hate to muddle
in a puddle
making bricks for you!"

Now one of of the children of God,
a man whose name was Moses,
saw a man from Egypt
whipping one of the slaves
working in the mud.

That made Moses angry
and he killed that cruel man.
But when the people said
that Moses was a murderer,
he quickly up and ran.

He ran across the hills
and he ran across the desert.
He ran across the marshes
and he ran across the sand,
until he came to a mountain.
There he found a strange old priest
watching his giggling goats.

Years went by and Moses learned
to like that strange old priest
with all his goats
who giggled at the lizards
in the hot desert sand.

Then one afternoon,
when the sun was burning hot
and the sky was burning hot
and the sand was burning hot,
a dry, old bush
caught on fire.

When Moses came near
he looked and he looked
and he couldn't believe his eyes.
The fire he saw
just flickered and glowed
in a strange and wonderful way.
It shone and glowed,
but nothing was burned away.
Nothing!
Nothing at all!

As Moses came nearer, someone spoke:
"Moses! Moses! This is no joke!"

Then Moses fell on his face in fear
and said, "I'm here! I'm here."

A voice came out of the bush again
and yelled, "Take off your shoes.
You're standing in front of God!"

So Moses stood without his shoes
on that burning yellow sand.

"Look. I am God," the voice went on,
"The God that Jacob knew.
I can hear the screams
of my people back in Egypt
trampling in the mud,
the slurpy mud,
the sloppy mud,
the slurpy, sloppy, soupy mud.

"Now I'm ready to take them home,
back to the land of Canaan,
and keep the promise I made to Jacob
a long time ago."

Moses stood there shaking
and wondering what to do,
as God cried out again:

"Be off now, Moses, go!
Tell the king of Egypt
to send My people home."

Moses kept spluttering something
like, "God, why ppppppick on mmmmmme?"

He tried to make excuses,
just the way we do.
But God kept saying, "Go!
Be off now, Moses, go!
I am with you always.
I'll show you what to do."

Moses spluttered something else
like, "God, You know I'm ttttttongue-tied.
I don't know wwwwwwhat to say."

But God kept saying, "Go.
Be off now, Moses, go!
I am with you always.
I'll tell you what to say."

Moses spluttered something else
and made some more excuses,
"God! We don't know who You are.
No one knows Your nnnnnnnnname!"

"I AM. I AM. I AM!"
said God, who was starting to shout.
"I AM with you always.
And if they ask My name,
just tell them all, I AM!
I AM WITH YOU.
I AM FOR YOU.
I AM ALL YOU NEED.
I AM. I AM. I AM.
Yes, that can be My name."

If you lived in Moses' day
you'd say that name, YAHWEH.
For that's the secret name of God,
the name that means HE IS.
HE IS WITH US ALWAYS
AND CAUSES THINGS TO HAPPEN
EVERYWHERE WE LIVE.

So Moses left his giggling goats
and mumbled to himself,
"HE IS. HE IS. YAHWEH. YAHWEH.
No one will believe me anyway."
But off he went
to tell the king of Egypt
to let God's people go.
For Moses was a special man
in God's purple puzzle plan.

OTHER TITLES

the PURPLE PUZZLE TREE